The SPIRIT of DECEPTION

Books by Tabitha Henton Lamb

The ReCreated Woman
How to Incorporate God's Plan into Your Life

Contending For the Faith
The Battleground of the Mind

God's Plan For Man

Strengthening Your Faith
Toolkit For the Believer

The Surrendered Life
A Pearl of Immense Value

Weathering Life's Storms
Equipping Yourself to Face the Challenges

Understanding God's Plan
Re-evaluating Your Relationship With God

The Purpose of Pain
How God Uses Pain to Strengthen Your Resolve

Enriching the Immortal Soul
A Journey Towards God
Available wherever online books are sold.

The
SPIRIT *of*
DECEPTION

How to Guard Against the Spirit of the Age

TABITHA HENTON LAMB

ISBN: 978-969-4292-93-9 Print

Contents

Introduction

The will of God is that none perish but that all men come to believe in Jesus. Since this is true, what do you suppose is the will of Satan against mankind? Pervert the will of God, and to cause men to do the exact opposite, of course. All of his attacks come with this intent, and his strategy is to deceive, just as in the beginning when Eve was deceived.

My dear reader, we cannot afford to be ignorant of the enemy's devices. We must expose his plan to oppose the plan of Jesus that all come to the knowledge of Him. He targets the mind to keep us from coming into the fullness of the knowledge of God. The Bible warns of false doctrine perpetuated by false prophets and teachers in these last days. Since the enemy comes to kill, steal, and destroy, all these false doctrines originate from him. The devil uses such false doctrines to set up and fortify strongholds of error.

One of his chief devices is to sow seeds of doubt in our minds. We sin when we doubt God and His word. How, you may ask? Because we choose not to believe His promises in a particular area. It's a lapse of faith in Jesus.

Therefore, it is essential that we fully understand the Gospel message, so our understanding is enlightened. The fundamental truth is that Jesus is the only way, the only truth, and the only life. All who come to the Father must go through Him, for He is the only one to grant us access to Father God. We must study the word of God to lay hold of His promises and show ourselves approved by God, able to rightly divide the word of Truth. He that comes to Jesus must first believe in Him. We do this when we accept His words as true without a shadow of a doubt.

Listen and take heed to the words of Jesus before He went to the cross. During this final intimate discourse with His disciples, Jesus revealed many things that were to come. He prepared them for His death, saying they would have sorrow—but only for a moment—but in the end they would receive everlasting joy. That joy would come from having a personal relationship with God through the Holy Spirit.

Jesus told them it was necessary for Him to go to the Father for the Holy Spirit to come. The Holy Spirit would come to execute Jesus' finished work on the cross, which was to build His church. In the coming persecution, the Holy Spirit would be their Comforter and Friend. He would work with them to reprove the world of sin, unrighteousness and judgment because Satan, the prince of this world, would be judged.

As the Spirit of Truth, the Holy Spirit would continue Jesus' work by leading them into all truth and bringing to remembrance the things they had been taught. He would not speak of Himself, but whatever He heard from the Father. His purpose on earth was to reprove, rebuke, reprise, reprimand, and admonish. Everything He did would be to glorify Jesus.

It is here that the disciples had a revelation of the mystery of the Father's plan from the beginning. They said to Him, "Now we believe that You know all things and there is no need for anyone to question You because of what You just revealed to us—the truth. By this we believe You came from God." Jesus replied, *"These things I have spoken unto you, that in me ye might have peace. In the world ye shall have tribulation: but be of good cheer; I have overcome the world"* (John 16:33).

Just as the Holy Spirit was with the early church, so is He with us in continuing the work of redemption. He is the intermediary between us and the Father, and the name of Jesus is our banner. Whatever we ask the Father in His name, He will give it to us. He assures us of the Father's love for us by giving us to the Father and the Father to us. The Father loves us because we love Jesus and acknowledge that He came from God.

In this book I will walk you through key areas that we often struggle with concerning our faith. They are submission of our own will to the will of the Father; the sinister nature of seducing spirits with their platter of "goodies;" the authority of our imagination in creating worlds of good or evil; our security in the righteousness of Jesus and not our own works; and finally, the life of promise when we are led by the Spirit and have a heart of gratitude for our Redeemer.

Chapter 1

THE GREAT SUBMISSION

The great submission in essence is all creation being subject to God. The universe, all spiritual beings, all of humanity, and all living things are designed to be in subjection to Him. This is the order of all creation and life forms including Heaven and Earth. However, some rebellious angels and humans opposed this divine order by altering their mission to a self-made one; thus they were separated from God.

That is why it is not until we deal with the issue of the lack of submission and rebellion, that we are empowered to participate in "The Great Submission." We must search out His word to come to know, and acknowledge the purpose of submission and our obligation. There is a reason and a purpose for it in God's plan.

Little research is needed to view our present world and what we have produced by the age-old spirit of rebellion.

This is the toddler's temper-tantrum way of showing his dislike for restriction. Due to his inability to process the larger scope of the world around him, man does not understand that his very safety and his protection are the reason for the boundaries God sets for us. Man does not see the timeless world around him consisting of the spirit realm. Although he lives in this world, he does not realize how being allowed his way in all things can be harmful to him.

This is precisely how humanity works against God, oblivious to the eternal dimension of life without the One who holds all things together. We fail to appreciate that we did not create ourselves or the universe but that He has graciously allowed us to discover this world. In his finite ability without God, man is incapable of governing the universe or ensuring his complete well-being. Unfortunately, many of us prefer to live independently of God thinking we know better. We demonstrate our rebellion in our pursuit of things for self-gratification—things like knowledge, power, and pleasure through inordinate desires. We want to have it all and persist in our all-consuming careers, unhealthy relationships, or dubious business practices, ignoring God's moral and spiritual laws.

On the other hand, we don't mind submitting to the ways of the world. We will undergo extensive training to learn about an organization's policies and procedures to secure employment. We will study their standard operating procedures to make sure we follow all the guidelines. However, when it comes to God, we pay little respect to what His word requires for the best possible life we can live, both now and in our spiritual resurrection. We build and secure our earthly retirement plans, yet our days are numbered on this earth and we have not done our due diligence to secure our spiritual retirement plan.

So is it to be a resurrection to life or a resurrection to death? If we could only grasp that our spiritual life and well-being are a choice of eternity with or without God, then we would have the eyes to see the value of life in its truest sense. The worldly choices become minute when we understand the true definition of life as spiritual. As with the spiritual life, so is it with the soul and physical life. It is the formula for the quality of life of all human beings.

Order in the Universe

The spiritual principle reveals that all of creation has internal boundaries established according to their purpose and use. The Universe has guidelines by which the planets exist and operate, the Sun by day and the Moon by night. The Sea has in place set boundaries by which its boisterous waves know their limits. The Earth is bound to remain suspended by gravity, to continue on its axis and to observe seed time and harvest. And what do we say about time? Time will remain but will move inexorably towards its ultimate mission, its date with eternity. Animal life is produced only after their kind. The Celestial and Terrestrial beings have their confines, as does all humanity. The Earth cannot take it upon itself to create a physical or a visible foundation to break its dependency on God who upholds all things, nor can the Heavens. All were created and instituted by God according to His will and good pleasure.

> *... for through him (Christ) God created everything in the heavenly realms and on earth. He made the things we can see and the things we can't see—such as thrones, kingdoms, rulers, and authorities in the*

unseen world. Everything was created through him and for him (Colossians 1:16 NLT, emphasis added).

Therefore, to understand our existence and purpose—the plan and purpose for humanity as a whole—we must go to the word of God who is Christ.

In the Beginning

In the beginning Adam and Eve were created as male and female in submission to God—to be a visible expression of God on Earth. Adam was the human expression of God in image and likeness. The Creator took the time to form him with intent and purpose to be the perfect picture of Himself. And so it was with Eve. He took the time to fashion her from the man, and for him. He took a rib from Adam and formed the woman to strategically complement the perfect design of Adam.

Woman is the true expression of what was inside of Adam. Adam called her *ishah* (woman) because she was "taken out of" his side. So Adam could say, *"This is now bone of my bones, and flesh of my flesh: she shall be called*

Woman, because she was taken out of Man" (Genesis 2:23).

Adam could also have added the following description of her: "She complements the part of me that is physically needed to reproduce and give life. With her, I can fulfill the commission by God to be fruitful and to multiply, to subdue and to replenish the Earth. I cannot fulfill that commission without her. For this reason, I am to love her as if she were my own body with a womb." The Bible goes on to say that a man is to leave his father and mother with their culture, traditions, and ways of doing things—abandon all of this—so that he can bind himself to a woman to fulfill God's integrative purpose. And the two shall become one flesh, not two entities but one, created and instituted by God from the beginning. That complementary role is still what He has established for humanity. It will require submission of the will, and the nature of man and woman to the will of God and to one another.

This is how God instituted the union of man and woman from the beginning: two persons but one flesh. God also is One in three persons in a blessed Trinity. *"The Lord our God is One"* (Deuteronomy 6:4). *"Hear O*

Israel, The Lord our God is one Lord, and you shall love the Lord your God with all of your heart, with all your soul and with all your mind" (Mark 12:29-31). Adam received the same gracious gift of life from God, while the woman is the delicate embodiment of the man, with the same honor bestowed upon her from God.

No other being has the same honor as man. I Peter 3:7 says that God crowned man with glory and with honor. And, David the psalmist could express with awe:

> *What is man, that thou art mindful of him? and the son of man, that thou visitest him?*

> *For thou hast made him a little lower than the angels, and hast crowned him with glory and honour.*

> *Thou madest him to have dominion over the works of thy hands; thou hast put all things under his feet …* (Psalm 8:4-5)

So the woman is the crowning glory of her husband—an honor to him.

A Collaborative Work

The Apostle John declares,

> *In the beginning was the Word, and the Word was with God and the Word was God. The same was true in the beginning with God. All things were made by Him, and without Him was not anything made that was made. (John 1:1)*

Compare this with the opening lines of Genesis:

> *In the beginning God created the heavens and the earth. And the earth was without form, and void; and darkness was upon the face of the deep. And the Spirit of God moved upon the face of the waters. And God said, Let there be light: and there was light (Genesis 1:1-3).*

We are immediately made aware God created the Heavens and the Earth when the Word (Jesus) spoke all creation into existence and the Spirit of God moved across the waters. Here we glimpse all of the Godhead in concert, the Father being the Chief Architecture, the Word declaring, and the Spirit bringing all into existence.

This wonderful collaboration is vividly elaborated in Proverbs by the Person called Wisdom, which I believe is one of the properties of the Triune God:

> *The* LORD *possessed me in the beginning of his way, before his works of old.*
>
> *I was set up from everlasting, from the beginning, or ever the earth was.*
>
> *When there were no depths, I was brought forth; when there were no fountains abounding with water.*
>
> *Before the mountains were settled, before the hills was I brought forth:*
>
> *While as yet he had not made the earth, nor the fields, nor the highest part of the dust of the world.*
>
> *When he prepared the heavens, I was there: when he set a compass upon the face of the depth:*

*When he established the clouds above:
when he strengthened the fountains of the
deep:*

*When he gave to the sea his decree, that the
waters should not pass his commandment:
when he appointed the foundations of the
earth:*

*Then I was by him, as one brought up with
him: and I was daily his delight, rejoicing
always before him;*

*Rejoicing in the habitable part of his earth;
and my delights were with the sons of* men
(Proverbs 8:22-31).

We see that Wisdom was with the Lord from the beginning, when He began His work in the universe. She held together His works both visible and invisible as the Godhead worked all things together in harmony.

In John 14, 15 and 16, Jesus makes it known that the Comforter would come. "I will send Him to you. He is the Spirit of Truth and will be sent from the Father. He will not testify of Himself, but He will testify of Me. He only works in unison and harmony with the Godhead, and has distinct roles and responsibilities. The Godhead is One. Outside of the Godhead, there is no peer, or one greater. Who is he who can oppose the hand of Almighty God? There is no one. All that exists was created by Him and for Him. There is nothing that exists outside of Him. Whatsoever is under the whole Heaven belongs to Him."

The same Holy Spirit of God that brought creation into existence by the Word of God is the same Holy Spirit that went with Jesus, the Word of God, when He descended to Earth. This same Spirit overshadowed Mary, causing her to conceive the Son of God in her womb. The same Spirit led Jesus into the wilderness to be tempted of the devil, and walked with Him throughout His days on earth. The same Spirit resurrected Him in the tomb.

Therefore, if God, the Supreme Being of all creation, can submit to Himself and make Himself available to humanity, what is our excuse for not submitting to Him? We are to be complete in Him just as we are to be complete in the essence and intended nature of our beings. This is our reward for His submission and obedience to the completion of the will of Father God. Jesus is now seated at the right hand of God with all power in Heaven and

Earth and below the Earth. At His second coming, after His one-thousand-year reign, He will hand all things over to the Father. He is an excellent exemplification of submission.

In John 17:5, Jesus prayed for glorification—both His own and the Father's. He asked to be glorified with Father God with His original glory, separate from His work on Earth, with the glory He had before He came into the world.

> *And now, O Father, glorify thou me with thine own self with the glory which I had with thee before the world was. I have manifested thy name unto the men which thou gavest me out of the world: thine they were, and thou gavest them me; and they have kept thy word (John 17:5-5).*

If we only wanted the original glory bestowed upon humanity by God, that would be enough for us! Jesus said that all He ever did was reveal the Father to us, for which He gave credit to God on His behalf. He spoke only words given to Him from God. He came only on the mission of Father God and not His own. *"For I have given unto them the words which thou gavest me"* to reveal the desire of the Father, *"And the glory which thou gavest me I have given them; that they may be one, even as we are one"* (John 17:21-22). What is this glory? That we may be one in God, perfect in Him; that the world may know He was sent from God and that He loves us just as He loves Jesus.

Jesus did not consider it robbery to willingly lay aside His majesty to submit to God's plan for our salvation. He made all of creation for Himself, and so He is responsible for all life forms on Earth for the well-being of all. Why then can we not submit ourselves to God and one another for the good of all of humanity? Look at the world around us. What have we gained from our quest for independence? The world is entirely corrupt, with humanity in bondage to its own will and desires. Why are we so consumed with altering the plan and purpose of what God created for Himself?

We are so consumed with that independence because Satan has beguiled us, just as he did Eve, to seek our own knowledge and become as gods (Genesis 3:5). This is the collision course we are on with God. Satan, in his rebellion against God, has set himself to destroy all of humanity. He knows we are the object of God's affection, made in His own image and placed above the angels in status. God's delight is with man. Why are we so bent on uniting ourselves with our enemy when we know that his prideful quest to be like God brought him to his fallen state, waiting for his eternal reward?

The conscience of humanity is so seared, we carry on blissfully, unaware of our state of reproach before our Creator. Just like Satan, man has succumbed to all manner of wickedness because of pride. If only we could search for the truth, to bring all forensic evidence into the courtroom of our mind before making a universal judgment against God! We and all our institutions have given over control to the "god" of this world, Satan. Do we realize that he controls the portals by which humanity receives knowledge? Through technology, he controls the airwaves and media platforms; through government, the political leaders and human agents; through the medical industry, the doctors and Big pharma; through religion, by counterfeit Christianity, false prophets and teachers; through the economy, all the worldly goods to awaken cravings for power and possessions; through entertainment, music, and culture, we are besieged with social enticements and inordinate pleasures.

In short, although the earth was made perfectly and habitable for humanity and all life forms, humanity rebelled and became corrupt, refusing to submit to God and His ways.

In the next chapter we will explore how man was beguiled into accepting Satan's world rather than God's perfect paradise. Deception is a formidable spirit.

Chapter 2

SEDUCING SPIRITS

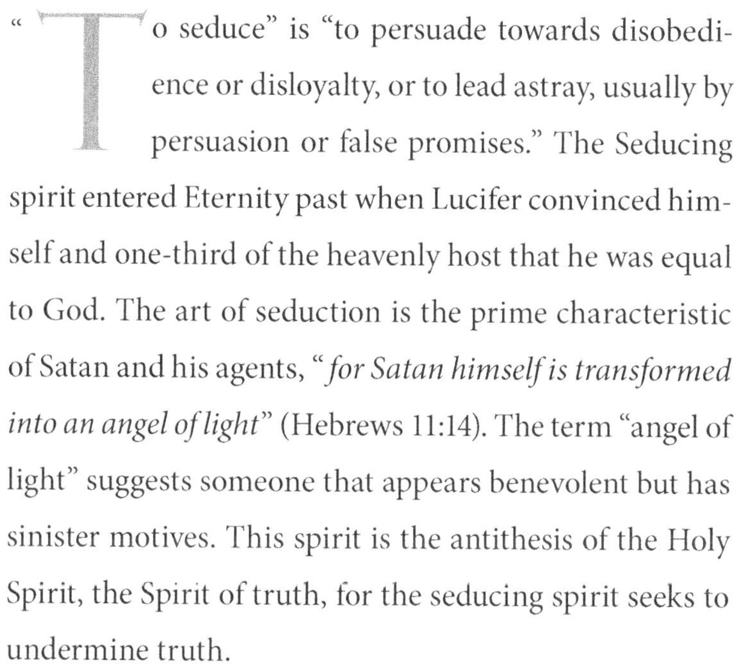

"To seduce" is "to persuade towards disobedience or disloyalty, or to lead astray, usually by persuasion or false promises." The Seducing spirit entered Eternity past when Lucifer convinced himself and one-third of the heavenly host that he was equal to God. The art of seduction is the prime characteristic of Satan and his agents, "*for Satan himself is transformed into an angel of light*" (Hebrews 11:14). The term "angel of light" suggests someone that appears benevolent but has sinister motives. This spirit is the antithesis of the Holy Spirit, the Spirit of truth, for the seducing spirit seeks to undermine truth.

In these last days, Joel 2:28 tells us that God will pour out His Spirit upon all flesh, and the gift of prophecy will be released upon young and old. It happened on the day of Pentecost for the early church (Acts 2:24) when God's Spirit was poured out, and signs, wonders and miracles were evident. It has happened in many global revivals throughout the ages, and will culminate in this end-time revival where there will be no denying the power of God. The Spirit of Truth will prevail over the minds and hearts of all of humanity and convict the hearts of many.

Deceptive Spirits Sent Out

But Satan is here to oppose the unveiling of the truth. The seducing spirit's mission is to pervert the truth in every aspect of society from individual beliefs to societal norms. He will attempt to subvert the truth just as he did with the heavenly host who followed him. It has been his mission for humanity since its very beginning. This angel of light has no new tricks to pull. Just as he beguiled Eve in the garden by not only deceiving her mind, but also by whetting her appetite for forbidden things, he will work his seductions on humankind through their sensuality and pride.

In these end times, this same spirit is infiltrating every sector of society especially education, the media, government and even the church. So devious is it that Jesus warned that the very elect, especially those who minister the Word, will be deceived: *"For there shall arise false Christs, and false prophets, and shall shew great signs and wonders; insomuch that, if it were possible, they shall deceive the very elect"* (Matthew 24:24).

Jesus' warning is so true in our day because, if the elect, who should know better are deceived, what will happen to the flock? We the people can no longer afford to trust what comes out of the pulpit as coming from God. Like the faithful Bereans in Paul's day who diligently searched the Word for confirmation of the apostles' teaching, we must put every teaching to the test by comparing it with what the Word says. As Apostle John told the early church, *"Beloved, believe not every spirit, but try the spirits whether they are of God: because many false prophets are gone out into the world"* (1 John 4:1).

The apostle Paul takes up the same theme with his disciple Timothy:

> *Now the Spirit speaketh expressly, that in the latter times some shall depart from the faith, giving heed to seducing spirits, and doctrines of devils; Speaking lies in hypocrisy; having their conscience seared with a hot iron ...* (1 Timothy 4:1-3)

Here again, it is ministers of the gospel who have fallen into apostasy by seducing spirits. Many will propagate false doctrines out of a lying heart, having lost their moral compass. We see this happening in the church today where many mainline denominations have sided with government in consenting to officiate same sex marriages, and condone abortions and gender fluidity.

What is the motive behind these sweeping changes that openly defy the Bible? The purpose is to nullify or distort the truth of God and turn it into a lie in the hearts of Christians. The intent is to lead humanity away from God without their realizing it. Seduction happens when we subtly add to or take away from the word of God and adopt these perverted doctrines of devils as our perceived truth. For example, the proponents of abortion avoid mention of the brutal fact of murdering an unborn child; instead, they set themselves up as champions of women's rights and the right of a woman to her own body. We must be mindful of changing the truth of His word to accommodate the agenda of civil society and even our own base motives. As Christians, our security and safety are in the word of God. When we distort the word of God, we become a law unto ourselves, and an open target for the kingdom of darkness.

In these latter days we are confronted by many false realities. We see them on display every day. Every time we turn on the news, we are not sure whether it's facts or propaganda being presented to lead us towards certain conclusions. But God knew everything before time began. He sent the Holy Spirit who leads us into all truth because He knew seducing spirits would arise to the extent of leading our own spiritual leaders astray. We are to heed the warnings of Jesus and the prophets concerning these perilous times. We need to stand in faith based on the incorruptible Word lest we fall—because those who give themselves over to seducing spirits will be enticed into great delusion. We are told in Romans 1:18-22 that those who choose to bind themselves to the lie rather than truth of God's word risk having their conscience seared. After that, there is no hope for conviction. When their minds are polluted by great deception, they can no longer be persuaded of the error of their ways. False doctrine has caused them to become apostate, exchanging the truth of God for a lie because they failed to uphold the truth.

My Encounter with Seducing Spirits

On December 1, 2023, I had a dream. The dream appeared to be a replay of an event that transpired earlier—the death of my mom. The house was not familiar, but the experience was. It appeared I was at my mom's house with her husband because she had just died. I came out of the bedroom with a blanket, a pen, and a notebook. I sat on a sectional-type sofa, covered myself, and positioned myself to write. Then a man came out of a room and sat next to me. He was too inappropriately dressed to be my mom's husband. Looking out of my peripheral vision, I noticed he was long, lean, and black.

My first thought was, "Oh, this is not what I thought it was!" Then I saw a man lying on the floor. I could hear his thoughts, "I won't leave her because something is wrong with this. I'm going to stay to make sure she is okay." So, he lay there pretending to be asleep. I saw him kicked repeatedly, but he would not move. I moved to the middle of the sectional, and I saw four men who were familiar to me on the floor. I remember thinking I was okay because I knew all of these men.

Then the scene seemed to transition. It was not a dream anymore: it was an experience. Still asleep, I found myself opposite where I initially sat. A bug was buzzing around my ear. Something or someone was sitting next to me. I could both feel and hear fear as it sprinkled over me. I did not feel it on the inside; it was coming from the outside.

I looked up, and the man who had come out of the room was now fully dressed in a tee shirt and shorts. He was now levitating in the air, horizontal on his side. In my mind I kept repeating these words, "The blood of Jesus is against you; the blood of Jesus is against you." However, I could not articulate the words because my lips were sealed. The tall, lean, and dark person sitting beside me was a spirit—I just knew it in my bones. He said, "Agents, stand up!" Immediately, two men—the most familiar or closest to me who were the only two lying face down— shifted onto their knees. They were covered with a wool-type of blanket that would be used to quench a fire or to shield oneself from a fire. I heard the evil spirit say, "My agents are everywhere," and I could hear myself repeat- edly saying, "The blood of Jesus is against you."

Interpretation

I believe the Holy Spirit used the dream to reveal the times in which we are living. I think the spirit portrayed in the men is a replica of the seducing spirit of this age. The covering is the same sort of covering intended to hide me from the truth or keep the truth from reaching the minds and hearts of the two men. Their conscience was so badly seared that even the conviction of the Holy Spirit could not penetrate them. I believe the men in the dream were men of God who had given themselves over to great delusion.

This dream is a true representation of the state of the body of Christ. The church has abandoned the truth of God for a lie and has sold its soul to the New Age grace movement and the prosperity gospel, along with many other false teachings.

The purpose of seducing spirits is to little by little influence us to fall away from the faith and the word of God. Those seduced by this spirit will eventually manifest a seared conscience as if pressed with a hot iron, numb and without moral sensitivity. Such people are coldly destructive and speak falsely and lie without a thought.

They have been drawn away from what they once upheld as the truth. Their mission is now to attack the truth and nullify it in the heart of the hearer. They work as influencers to present the truth as false, and falsehood as truth just as Satan misled the heavenly host and Eve. Now convinced of their rightness, no conscience or conviction is available to them any longer, for Hebrews 10:26 tells us that if we deliberately continue sinning after we have received knowledge of the truth, there is *no longer* any sacrifice that will cover these sins.

The seducing spirit has positioned them to be open to all evil and they are on the way to accomplishing his goal—total deception of the soul. The truth of God is now void and made a lie.

How the Elect Can Be Deceived

I want to bring up a story in the Old Testament to highlight the subtlety of seduction. Do you remember the man of God whom God sent to Bethel to prophecy against King Jeroboam because of his idolatry? (1 Kings 13) This man of God had strict instructions not to eat or drink at anyone's house, and to not leave by the same way he had entered the city. God had prepared him to resist any seducing spirits lurking in the area, and he had to leave a different way so as not to be noticed.

The man of God successfully completed the mission and left the city. However, an invitation came to him from an old prophet who lived in the city to turn back and dine with him. The old prophet pretended he had received a message from an angel for him to return and eat with him. He lied. At first the man of God declined the invitation, reiterating the precise instructions from God about not stopping to eat with anyone and taking another route home. However, after a little persuasion from the old prophet, he relented in deference to the elder's title; he visited his house, and dined with him.

Ironically, the same prophet who summoned him to his house now receives a word from the LORD foretelling the destruction that would come to this man of God because of his disobedience. Moreover, he would not be buried in his ancestral burial place. The man of God did indeed meet with a horrific death that same day. A lion accosted him on the road and mauled him to death. Strangely enough, the lion did not eat the man or attack his donkey but both the lion and the donkey stood quietly beside the man's body. The old prophet mourned this tragic death caused by him and, ironically, he who seduced him was the one to bury him in his own tomb.

False instructions were sent to destroy the man of God and they succeeded. He thought he had accomplished his mission by delivering the message to the king, and his guard was down. But the mission was not over until he completed his journey. He was not afraid to confront the king about his sin but he gave in to the old prophet because of his "spiritual" seniority.

Surely this is a grave lesson to us to follow the word of the Lord exactly as it is given! We are reminded that we are in constant warfare and must always be vigilant against deception. If we were, we would not be taken up by the persuasive words of a minister which are in conflict with the word of God, no matter how high his office. Often, it is after a great battle that we sit back and relax, and that is when the enemy launches his real attack. He works behind the scenes to see who he can devour.

That God could magnify His Word over and above his very name (Psalm 138:2), shows the supremacy of the Word over all things. This is so important that Paul could tell the Galatians, *"But though we, or an angel from heaven, preach any other gospel unto you than that which we have preached unto you, let him be accursed"* (Galatians 1:8). It's so important that the angel could rebuke John the revelator for bowing down before him, saying, *"See you do it not: for I am your fellow-servant, and of your brethren the prophets, and of them which keep the sayings of this book: worship God"* (Revelation 22:9). In fact, this was the second time John did it. It seemed the natural human thing to do at the sheer wonder of such a majestic being out of whose mouth came such powerful revelations. But the word expressly forbids us to worship anyone or anything in the universe other than the Creator God: *"For thou shalt worship no other god: for the* Lord, *whose name is Jealous, is a jealous God ..."* (Exodus 34:14)

Agents of Satan

The seducing spirit works through men as advocates or agents of Satan himself, stumbled by their own ignorance, avarice or pride into great delusion. They go about deceived in their conscience. Because they have walked away from the love of God, they have no remorse. Their pursuit is to pull others from their place in God out of the will of God, and there is great pleasure at the destruction of their victims. Dominated by a seducing spirit, they can sometimes be misled into believing they are working for God as they swiftly apprehend their prey, contaminate their thought life, and gain dominance over that soul.

The seducing spirit works through the mind to manifest rebellion against God. It performs its best when unforgiveness, anger, and hate go unchecked, and there is no restraint over what we communicate. It is not that some don't believe in Jesus, but their deeds are evil. Rather than be convicted, they do not want to turn away from their errors, and slowly but surely their conscience is seared. "How wonderful to find acceptance!" they say—in the board room, in that newspaper, in that political party that denies the lordship of Christ! The fool has said there is no God in his heart and men, forsaking the light, run to the darkness and find themselves in the territory of seducing spirits and doctrines of devils. Loose talk and mocking words about the God of Creation and the Savior of our souls are their breeding grounds. James warns that if any man does not bridle his tongue but deceives his own heart, this man's outward show of righteousness is futile.

We saw earlier how in the last days, some will depart from the faith, giving heed to seducing spirits and doctrines of devils (I Timothy 4:11). They will depart from the faith because they are seeking to justify their show of pride, unforgiveness, bitterness, resentment, and holding onto grudges. That opens the door to seducing spirits. If you have not given your heart entirely over to Jesus and received His unconditional love, you are a prime target for a seducing spirit. It is when the human mind seeks to condone what God forbids that we are left at the mercy of the enemy. We must find it in our heart to remain faithful to the word of God because it is our lifeline against all evil. A seducing spirit will always cause us to justify our operating in whatever appetite we want to gratify.

Test the Spirits

We must walk in love at all costs and allow Jesus to be the judge of everything in the turbulent times ahead. Those overtaken by these spirits will not hear or believe the truth. They are combative and argumentative and only have itching ears for novelty. But we must proceed with caution, testing all spirits to discern if they are of God or of the evil one before we believe their message. We are to know no man after the flesh but only the Spirit. If the message or prophecy does not line up with the Word, then it is not of God.

On the other hand, the doctrine of Satan is always contrary to the word of God. This is his end-time strategy against the church to cause a great falling away from the truth. He typically works through the ones we respect, love, and trust. Take Adam, for instance. Can you imagine how he must have felt to know that the woman given by God was the one Satan would use to seduce him into wrongdoing? Can you imagine the betrayal and hurt? But, even though he knew it was wrong, he cherished her companionship more than the sweet companionship of God in the cool of the day. This is the same unfortunate story of the many who were seduced by loved ones or those who they trusted as spiritual leaders, not realizing their hidden agenda was to manipulate, control, or dominate others for their devious motives.

What is the message of the seducing spirit? It is governed by the doctrine of demons based on false doctrines, untruths or distortions. The purpose is to promote disloyalty. It floods the mind with untruths that appeal to human reasoning that is not turned over to Jesus. To guard our heart against its seductions, we must take care to let this mind be in us that is in Christ Jesus. The path to continuous peace is to fix our gaze on Jesus, and thereby escape the mental sorrow the affairs of this world bring. Meditate on the things that are noble and true and lovely, not nursing bitterness or offense. These are simply opportunities for Satan to capitalize on, making us susceptible to his work.

There is a way that seems right to a man, but its end is destruction. It's the broad path that leads to destruction, but it's the narrow path that leads to life. Few find the narrow path because of the isolation and sacrifice it often entails; but many find the broad path of popularity and success, even in the church. But God gives to each of us a shield of defense and protection—*"His truth shall be your shield and buckler"* (Psalm 91:4). But we must first want to be kept by Him. Our problems begin and end with our failure to continue believing in Jesus to be our all in all. He will keep us in perfect peace when we keep our minds on Him (Isaiah 26:3). When we give Him all our love in word and deed, His love will cover a multitude of faults. We are safe in Christ if we trust the path He has secured for us.

Sadly, there will be many believers who will not enter the kingdom of Heaven. These are the tares mingled with the wheat that look so alike, they grow unnoticed in the same environment—maybe in the same household, maybe the same church! However, there will be a great separation at the end of the age when the tares are exposed, and cast into the fire. It is only those that love the Lord with a genuine heart, and abide in the His Word that will flourish and thrive.

In the next chapter we will look at the role of the imagination in relation to our faith.

Chapter 3

IMAGINATION'S AUTHORITY

What is it about the imagination to make it so powerful? What was in the mind of God when He gave us this creative faculty? Let's look at a few scriptures to see if we can identify the intent. Let's look at the first scripture in which God revealed the imagination and the power behind it.

> *And the LORD said, Behold, the people is one, and they have all one language; and this they began to do: and now nothing will be restrained from them, which they have imagined to do* (Genesis 11:6).

A vivid imagination seized the people to build the tower of Babel to reach the heavens, and thus they became united in intent and ambition. The question is, was their imagination working for them or against them?

We can at once see that the imagination can have good and bad intent. On the one hand, it spurs us on to believe and put on faith in God, and it helps us to visualize who we were recreated to be in Christ. Here are some examples of positive imagination.

Ephesians 3:20:

> *Now to Him who is able to do exceedingly abundantly above all that we ask or think, according to the power that works in us.*

This verse looks to the limitless power of God to exceed our expectations and imagination. When we use our imaginations according to God's will and power, this can lead to amazing outcomes beyond what we ever dreamed of.

Philippians 4:8:

> *Finally, brethren, whatsoever things are true, whatsoever things are honest, whatsoever things are just, whatsoever things are pure, whatsoever things are lovely, whatsoever things are of good report; if there be*

*any virtue, and if there be any praise, think
on these things.*

Here we are encouraged to meditate on things that are lovely and praiseworthy. That means using our imagination to reflect on the good things in life, and in so doing develop a grateful heart and a positive outlook.

Hebrews 11:1:

*Now faith is the substance of things hoped
for, the evidence of things not seen.*

This verse suggests that our faith can be fueled by our God-given imagination. It encourages us to use our imagination to creatively visualize the fulfillment of God's promises, and thus build up our faith.

On the other hand, the imagination can and will work against us if we allow it to run rampant without boundaries. So in the tower of Babel verse we just cited, we learn the destructive power of imagination. God saw its potential for evil and knew the people had discovered the power of imagination, not for His intended purpose but their desire for self glory. He therefore decided to scatter them because their ambition and their misuse of the power of unity would know no bounds:

> *And the* Lord *said, "Behold, they are one [unified] people, and they all have the same language. This is only the beginning of what they will do [in rebellion against Me], and now no evil thing they imagine they can do will be impossible for them"* (Genesis 11:6 AMP).

Imagination is the mental faculty to form ideas, or images or concepts of external objects not externally present but derived from reality. It is the predisposition to act on what we have been thinking. Unchecked thoughts turn into unbridled imaginations, while imagination is safe as long as it remains within godly boundaries of reasonable behavior. However, once it is allowed to run wild in its ruminations, the imagination turns into a stronghold capable of controlling your life. Strongholds are beliefs or opinions opposed to the word of God. These strongholds are formed in our mind and are fiercely guarded by us. When we harbor such thoughts as denial of God's authority, rebellion, lust and rejection, we are inviting demonic entry to control our life.

So random thoughts create our imagination, and uncontrolled imaginations develop into strongholds. There are three primary ways to feed our thought life. The first is through our internal recollections from the past, our present, familiar surroundings, and our upbringing. The second is thoughts and suggestions fed to us by Satan through fear or temptations. The third is by God through our born-again spirit. There is a strategy for the human mind to guide its thought life and that is to fill it with godly wisdom and wholesome thoughts. We develop this when we meditate on the Word, allowing it to take root and produce a healthy and productive thought life.

How is it you ask that we can have ungodly thoughts when we are born again? We must remember that we are three-part beings consisting of spirit, soul (mind, will and emotions) and body. When we are saved, it is our spirit that comes alive and reaches for the things of God. Our soulish nature has to learn the things of God and be renewed. So we have the choice of being led by the Spirit of God, in other words, dominated by our spirit or we can continue to be dominated by our old unregenerate nature. When the old nature leads, it impedes our spiritual growth because it is controlled by the senses with all their feelings and sensual appetites. But if we allow ourselves to be moved according to the leading and guidance of the Holy Spirit—we will be led into all truth, as the word of God regenerates our born-again spirit.

The Carnal Mind

The old nature or way of living is dead, and the new nature is alive in Christ. The old processes are no longer the way to life and peace. They come to dull the mind and cause it to be receptive to the negative transmissions coming across from Satan. While the Spirit-filled mind leads to life, the carnal sense- dominated mind leads to death.

> *For those who live according to the flesh*
> *set their minds on the things of the flesh,*
> *but those who live according to the Spirit,*
> *the things of the Spirit. For to be carnally*
> *minded is death, but to be spiritually*
> *minded is life and peace. Because the car-*
> *nal mind is enmity against God; for it is*
> *not subject to the law of God, nor indeed*

can be. So then, those who are in the flesh cannot please God (Romans 8:5-8).

Our carnal mind prompts our imagination to work in this way. When we feel an impression, our first response is generally to acknowledge it and often to speak it out. As we begin to entertain it further with little understanding of where it came from, it will create our reality. This happens because we begin to agree with the thought. For example, when we do not feel well, we typically say, "I feel sick," or "I have the flu coming on," and with a little imagination this can expand to "I've caught the virus. Maybe it was from the crowd at that meeting." What did you just say? You felt something and let your imagination run with it. Your carnal mind did that rather than to immediately reject the thought, and renew the mind to make the right declaration from the word of God in the situation.

You could say, "I feel sick but I take authority over sickness and declare that by the stripes of Jesus I am healed! Lord, thank You for sending Your word to heal me! I command every disease, and every weakness in my body to leave me, in Jesus' name!" Here's another one, "I feel afraid." Instead of expressing the reality that you feel the spirit of fear, we tend to own what we feel. No, keep it separate long enough to discern what triggered the thought. What took place at that moment? Then cast out the thought. Say, "Spirit of fear, I command you to leave me now, in Jesus' name. Lord, thank You for giving me the spirit of power, love and of a sound mind. Fear, I rebuke you; get out of my life!"

Walking in the Law of Life

We now live according to the new nature, the law of life in Christ Jesus. Romans 8:1 says, *"For the law of the Spirit of life in Christ Jesus has made me free from the law of sin and death."* We go through the process of being under the law of life when we renew our minds. It's an ongoing process because of the resistance from the old self. When we empty the old way of thinking and doing things and put on the new life in Christ, the old nature will still want to exercise its natural reactions to situations through emotions of fear, panic, anger and confusion. However, the new man will position us to respond to all things according to the Word. When we move away from the normal impulses of the old nature, we can learn to face and deal with things patiently and calmly.

> *For though we walk in the flesh, we do not war after the flesh (For the weapons of our warfare are not carnal, but mighty through God to the pulling down of strong holds ...)*
> (2 Corinthians 10:3-4)

We must therefore pull down strongholds in our thought lives and the imaginations they create. This is the stand we take:

> *Casting down imaginations, and every high thing that exalteth itself against the knowledge of God, and bringing into captivity every thought to the obedience of Christ ...* (2 Corinthians 10:5)

The renewal process is to identify the situation and to hold the thought presented. Do not react presumptively. Suspend the thought long enough to identify it. Hold it captive to the obedience of Christ by bringing it under subjection to obey Christ. You hold the thought captive long enough to use the Word to replace it.

These thoughts with their vivid imaginations, motives and agendas are all driven by the carnal mind or five senses. Corruption or perversion of the Word is their name and destruction is their destination. What you rehearse over and over in your mind and imagination eventually becomes your reality: *"For as he thinketh in his heart, so is he"* (Proverbs 23:7). Your imagination is a fertile ground for sowing seeds of destruction. To create a stronghold for whatever it is, we are the ones who give it repeated thoughts.

It is essential to pay attention to our wandering thoughts because we are led or driven by what we offer our thoughts to. What we think about is what we will meditate on. What we meditate on becomes what we do. Suppose you allow the wrong thoughts into your mind. Once this process is in operation, you will be consumed by what you have given your thoughts to. Not long after you will see the outward manifestation of what you meditated on from its conception to the reality of what you imagined. It has become a stronghold.

Think of the results if you use the same process with the Word? If you feed your mind on the Word of God and allow it to accept Christ's thoughts, and have the

mind of Christ, it will receive these thoughts and meditate on them until godly imagination takes place. Where
the enemy's strongholds come into play with the carnal
mind, your sonship under the lordship of Christ come
into place fortified with the Word. A new man lives on
the inside of you.

We must learn to guard our minds. All things are
possible through Christ, who strengthens you. We must
learn to have only the kind of thoughts that mirror the
mind of Christ. This is possible when we fill our minds
and hearts with only the Word. It is the only way to keep
the heart pure and whole without being offended or causing offense. Remember, the natural is being pitted against
the supernatural, and the supernatural must win. Outside
of this, we are open to the entrapment of the carnal mind
with its futile reasoning that negates all of what Jesus
came to deliver us from. We free our hearts and minds by
renewing our thoughts, casting everything that opposes
the law of life down, and bringing every thought to the
obedience of Christ.

Therefore, determine not to allow your imagination to
have its way but intentionally meditate on the things that
are pure, lovely, and of excellent report (Philippians 4:8).

To give focus and attention to these kinds of thoughts, we must learn to make the exchange immediately. The word of God gives us the power to entertain no opposing thought to the word, to pull down strongholds, and to cast down imaginations. Therefore, to exercise the right of refusal, replace the distorted truth with the genuine truth of the Word, and separate and detach it from the reality of your mind.

Imagination is your ability to see something not visible or present. You see in the spirit what is to be in the natural but you must see it yourself. Do not be afraid to imagine what God has for you and what He has planned for your life. Your mind is where you conceive it, and where it is conceived and cultivated it becomes your reality. It will not become your reality if you do not use it. If you can imagine according to God's plans and desires for you, nothing will be impossible for you. You must yourself cast down vain imaginations that exalt themselves above your reality of who God says you are, and you must choose to dwell on the right imagery. See yourself loved by your Father, secure and successful according to Ephesians 3:20. What we think paints the canvas of our imagination. We must guard it with great care and fill it with what it produces—faith.

Therefore beware of Satan's subtle devices. Even the most innocent thoughts or statements may not be what they appear to be when you consider the source or originator. For example, when someone dabbling in horoscopes wishes you success, reject that blessing immediately because the enemy has no good will towards you. Every word must be tested and approved on the basis of the Word before entry. Every feeling must be God approved and God tested. If it is not accompanied with peace, it is not from God. If your joy or peace is compromised, reject the thought or feeling. Train your mind to sense and discern each feeling.

The Word of God brings light as it enters your mind; it is a lamp to our feet and a light to our pathway. Jesus said, *"Man shall not live by bread alone but by every word out of the mouth of God"* (Luke 4:4). This is the confidence for us, absolute dependency on the word of God. No guile in the heart. No hidden motives or agendas. No secret compartments to store things. Only absolute dependency. There is no need to prove you can be enticed by temptation and not be overtaken by it, unless there is some unrighteousness in you so that you need to prove who you are. No, resist the enemy and his enticing words, and he will flee.

If we only understood the truth about the unseen realm we would know there is no gray area! Either we will be dominated and governed by the Spirit of God, or we will be dominated and controlled by Satan. It is to whom we yield our members that determines who is lord over us. You will know the tree by the fruit. Persistent un-controlled thoughts and imaginations form strongholds that prohibit us from walking in truth and obedience to God and His word. No excuses or justifications are ever a reason to be disobedient to His word. It is not worth the damage and destruction that await the soul that is lured by the bait of Satan.

So how is our identity influenced by our culture and social customs?

Chapter 4

AMBIENT IDENTITY

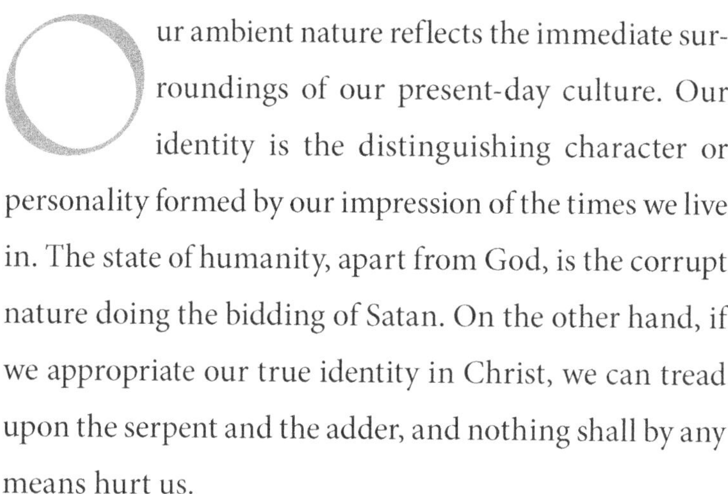

Our ambient nature reflects the immediate surroundings of our present-day culture. Our identity is the distinguishing character or personality formed by our impression of the times we live in. The state of humanity, apart from God, is the corrupt nature doing the bidding of Satan. On the other hand, if we appropriate our true identity in Christ, we can tread upon the serpent and the adder, and nothing shall by any means hurt us.

However, our human nature often wants the blessings without the qualifiers. However, there are qualifiers for the blessings of the covenant in Christ when we follow the law of Christ (Galatians 6:2).

Recognizing False Identifiers

The man who expects to live a life of unimpeded blessing opens himself to the entry of what I call "false identifiers." These are characteristics that are associated with our lower base nature and not with our identity as new creations in Christ. How do we recognize these false identifiers? Through the word of God. They are false in appearing to be the thing denoted but are not; they are deliberately meant to deceive. They produce a false report, not according to truth or fact but with distorted or inaccurate information. We are always to test the spirit behind the report, that is, the person or a thing that it can be identified with.

We must first recognize the false identifiers to know where they are hiding. The next step is to discover why they are present. We can sometimes be so thirsty for great revelations to fill our itching ears, we do not recognize the hidden agendas behind any news. My friends, be wary because this is the hour of great deception. Therefore we must be trained to use the word of God and discern what deception paraded as truth is coming at us. In this hour of fake news and fear, the response of the church should always be to counter error with truth and faith.

The gift of comprehending the light of God's word came to us when we received the Spirit of Truth. We must learn to exercise the gift of discerning spirits to its fullest capacity and we must remain rooted in the word. We must become so identified with Christ through His death, burial, resurrection, and life that we do not need outside measures to define us.

Although we live in a material world, the truth is that we are governed more by the spirit realm than the natural. As it goes in the spirit, so is it in the natural. If the Bible says, *"the weapons of our warfare are not carnal, but mighty through God to the pulling down of strong holds"* (2 Corinthians 10:4), then this life is a spiritual life with spiritual battles, and spiritual enemies for spiritual purposes. The ruler of darkness projects to the rulers of this world his weapons to unleash upon humanity for his sinister purposes. Whether it's through blatant evil, politics, clever inventions, food, material things, viruses—you name it—they are invented for the downfall of society as a whole. How so? There is always some new invention or gadget, latest trend, new drug, new forms of power, and novel pleasure; but note that all are designed to keep humanity bound to carnal desires to satisfy our craving for possessions, knowledge, and power. By design, the continuous cycle of novelties makes it impossible for us to be satisfied.

Satan's intent is to play to this evil bent in our character to bring us to ultimate ruin. He is seeking to destroy our souls. He is unable to target his stealthy acts on God because God has no vulnerabilities, so we, the apple of His eye, are his next best option. We have only to look at the seed of unforgiveness to see how this seed can evolve into an all-consuming evil in so many lives. But there is a higher quality of life that allows us to live above our human tendencies, human reasoning and conscientiousness. It's God Consciousness. God Consciousness will permit us to live above it all. We can enjoy the pure quality of life promised by Jesus, which is made available through the work of the Holy Spirit.

Another Prophetic Dream

On September 4, 2023, I had what I will describe as a dream and an encounter. A person familiar to me was at my home. After he walked out, I noticed the money that was on the counter was no longer there. When he walked back in, I inquired about it, and he responded he did not have it. I said to him that he did. He put the money back on the counter; however, I did not believe it to be all the money. He walked out again, and when he did, this is when it transitioned from a dream to an encounter.

I heard keys in the door, and the door opened. I heard the keys drop on the wall table. I saw a black spirit grab a chair near the wall and pull it to the door of my bedroom. As he was watching me, I was calling upon the blood of Jesus. Then I found myself in a body of water like a sea or an ocean. As I was fighting the water, trying to surface to the top, some force restrained me. It was bent on trying to pull me down. To my left, I saw a long black spirit. A forearm from the elbow to the hand formed out of the water. The hand grabbed me and pulled me to what seemed like the abyss of the sea. But I was still saying, "The blood of Jesus is against you!" I quickly realized this force apparently had gained some foothold in me.

At this point, I cried as loud as I could with everything inside of me, "I belong to Jesus!" When I did, it roared and thundered through the waters, and whatever had a hold on me broke. That spirit was mad and angry. Now I began to soar in and with the water like I became one with it. As I soared, I began to sing a new song to the Lord. Finally, I made it to the shore. This place was like an island. My clothes were completely dry. I was walking in search of a particular building. I saw people I was familiar with. When it was time for me to leave, I had to go back into the water. I struggled to get back, but I began to soar again, and as I did, I sang a different new song to the Lord.

Interpretation

I believe the dream represents a person I was familiar with who came to visit. When they were unable to keep all that was stolen, they tried to have revenge on me, and the black image that took a seat, sat as a watcher. The force or hand that opposed me in the water was in union with the water just as I was, but it had a stronger hold than me. I saw the image take shape, so I was aware of what was happening. I recognized the enemy had something on me because there was no reason the blood of Jesus should not have worked. Whatever it was, it lost control or its ability to hold me once I discovered something was there and bound myself to Jesus. With my "I belong to Jesus" cry, came freedom and deliverance from whatever this was.

What were coming against me, both the water and the hand, lost control: the hand disappeared, and I literally became one with the water. The water no longer worked against me but was now in unison with me. I literally soared from the depths of the water.

I believe this dream to exemplify the identifiers that are hidden and unseen in our lives. We give them access when we either operate in things that have familiar spirits or when we are in close proximity with a familiar spirit through others. I knew that the Blood of Jesus would be both my defense and my weapon against this enemy. When it did not work, I also recognized it pointed to something in me that was hidden from my human mind and heart. It is not until I gave total surrender and allegiance to Jesus that the power of this hand broke and it lost its hold. Everything demonic had to go.

One of the most effective prayers outside of the salvation prayer is to ask God to allow us to see what hold the enemy has on us. If we ask this with a sincere heart and a commitment to release it to Him, He will reveal it to us. That is the only reason the word of God will not work in our lives and situations. We must get to the place of being empty of all our baggage to be filled completely.

Some False Identifiers

Let us take a look at a few false identifiers that try to define us. The first one is pride.

Pride

Pride is taking the glory that belongs to God. Pride rears its head at every opportunity to exalt oneself. We should acknowledge that all good things belong to God, for the Bible says all good and perfect gifts are from above (James 1:17). If there is a good thing in us, it comes from God alone. All gifts, skills, unique talents, or admirable characteristics are all of Him, and for that we must give Him glory.

Now, the word of God is clear about not sharing His glory with anyone, neither man nor angel. *"I am the LORD: that is my name: and my glory will I not give to another, neither my praise to graven images"* (Isaiah 42:8). Pride is the fastest way to becoming an enemy with Him.

God resisteth the proud, but giveth grace unto the humble. Submit yourself, there-fore, to God. Resist the devil, and he will flee from you. Draw nigh to God, and he will draw nigh to you. Cleanse your hands, ye sinners, and purify your hearts, ye double minded. Be ye afflicted, mourn, and weep: let your laughter be turned to mourning and your joy to heaviness (James 4:6-9).

The fear of the LORD is to hate evil, pride, arrogance and the evil way, and a froward mouth, do I hate (Proverbs 8:13).

These six things doth the LORD hate: yea, seven are an abomination unto him: A proud look, a lying tongue, and hands that shed innocent blood, An heart that deviseth wicked imaginations, feet that be swift in running to mischief, A false witness that speaketh lies, and he that soweth discord among brethren (Proverbs 6:16-19).

Every one that is proud in heart is an abomination to the LORD: though hand join in hand, he shall not be unpunished (Proverbs 16:5).

A man's pride shall bring him low: but honor shall uphold the humble in spirit (Proverbs 29:23).

Pride goes ahead of destruction, and a haughty spirit guarantees a fall. It is not a characteristic that we, as believers, should entertain. Pride is detestable to Him. It is not a fruit of His God-given Spirit. What is the proper identifier for our God-given identity in place of pride? Humility. Humility is an admirable characteristic before God, one that is pleasing, and one He will accept. Humility proceeds honor. He who makes himself low before God is the one God will find trustworthy enough to promote, saying, "Friend, go up higher" (Luke 14:10).

Satan tested Jesus during the temptation in the wilderness by questioning His trustworthiness before Father God. The path to honor in God's kingdom is humility. While pride exalts the self, humility exalts God. Honor in the kingdom of God is for service, not for prideful self-seeking.

Fear

The next false identifier is the spirit of fear. Fear is a normal response to danger because it gives us the stamina for flight or fight. But when one's entire life is dominated by fear, then we know that the spirit of fear has entered the person and must be cast out.

The antidote to the spirit of fear is God's perfect love; this wraps itself around us like a mantle and is powerful enough to cast out any kind of fear. The Bible says, *"There is no fear in love; but perfect love casteth out fear: because fear hath torment. He that feareth is not made perfect in love"* (1 John 4:18).

His perfect love for us has been evident since Genesis 3:15, where He promises us the seed of the woman—a Savior. The seed was His Beloved Son sent into the world, not to judge or to condemn but to save. It is the antidote to fear. He saved us before we were even sinners or before we could do any wrong, simply because of His covenant with Himself concerning humanity. From the beginning of time, He chose to redeem us. It was a radical plan but He had made provision for our failure knowing we would rebel, deny Him, and crucify Him. He knew we would attempt to exalt ourselves, and use His resources to furnish our quest to live without Him. Yet, He still came and died for us. The Lamb, slain before the foundation of the world, is our remedy for every kind of tormenting fear, for fear involves tormenting spirits. With this truth, we can stand solidly in His perfect love, and reassure ourselves whenever we fall short.

Know that He loves the sinner but He hates sin. There is not one thing we can do that will cause His love to turn away from us even when we choose to live apart from Him. Those who continue to reject Him until their final breath, will be tormented for eternity when they realize His love was ever present even in the midst of their rebellion. Eternity in Hell is outside of Him and His love. No more opportunity is available for mercy or grace. You will know it, feel it, and understand it. However, it will be too late to be reconciled to Him. But for now, He has made every provision for the sinner's return. He is longsuffering, not willing that any should perish but all to come to repentance. He is a gentleman, and will not impose His will upon anyone. He simply invites anyone who is thirsty and wishes to take the free gift of the water of life to come (Revelation 22:17).

Unforgiveness

Unforgiveness is another false identifier. Unforgiveness separates us from Jesus. It is one of the adversary's best weapons of entrapment.

The spiritual principle of reciprocity concerning forgiveness enables us to walk in our new identity in Christ. *"Bear with each other and forgive one another if any of you has a grievance against someone. Forgive as the Lord forgave you"* (Colossians 3:13 NIV).

For some of us, the process begins by receiving true forgiveness from God for wronging Him. If God indeed forgives us, what right have we to withhold it from others? A closer look is required if we are struggling in this area. Forgiveness is a spiritual privilege we receive by faith from God, and we are to extend it to others. As the Lord has forgiven us, so are we to forgive others. We are new creatures in Christ, and unforgiveness goes against our new nature in Him. Never convince yourself you need or deserve to harbor unforgiveness, hatred, bitterness, or resentment against another.

These are key scriptures to meditate on when you are challenged in the area of unforgiveness and related areas like judgmental attitudes, anger and revenge.

Forgiveness:

And forgive us our debts, as we forgive our debtors (Matthew 6:12).

> *For if ye forgive men their trespasses, your heavenly Father will also forgive you. But if ye do not forgive men their trespasses, neither will your Father forgive your trespasses* (Matthew 6:14-15).

> *And when ye stand praying, forgive, if ye have ought against any: that your Father also which is in heaven may forgive you your trespasses* (Mark 11:25).

Jesus tells the story of a servant who was forgiven his great debt, but refused to forgive a fellow servant who owed him a small amount. This so angered his master that he "*delivered him to the tormentors, till he should pay all that was due unto him.*" Jesus said His heavenly

Father would do the same to us, if we do not genuinely forgive others who wrong us (Matthew 18:34-35). Those tormentors could give us perpetual unrest that could lead to mental disorders and chronic diseases.

Judgmental tendencies:

> *Judge not, and ye shall not be judged: condemn not, and ye shall not be condemned: forgive, and ye shall be forgiven (Luke 6:37).*

Anger: it is not a sin to be angry but it becomes a sin when you hold on to it.

> *Be ye angry, and sin not: let not the sun go down upon your wrath: Neither give place to the devil (Ephesians 4:26-27)*

Revenge:

> *Dearly beloved, avenge not yourselves, but rather give place unto wrath: for it is written, Vengeance is mine; I will repay, saith the Lord. Therefore if thine enemy hunger, feed him; if he thirst, give him drink: for in*

> *so doing thou shalt heap coals of fire on his*
> *head. Be not overcome of evil, but overcome*
> *evil with good (Romans 12:19-21).*

When we rejoice at the mishaps of others, it could be a sign of revenge:

> *Do not rejoice when thine enemy falleth,*
> *and let not thine heart be glad when he*
> *stumbleth (Proverbs 24:17).*

False identifiers surface as a sign we are not firmly sealed in Christ. We can identify their fruit in various ways, from medical diagnoses: high blood pressure, Chron's disease, diabetes, cancer, heart disease to the propensity towards lust, depression, or low self-esteem. These are conditions we commonly accept as hereditary, saying they run in the family. What they do reveal is the intrusion of a generational curse or a familiar spirit *in a life not hidden in Christ.* When they surface, it is an opportunity to search out and discover its point of entry or access.

You will find this flaw hidden in the soul life more than the physical or the natural. It is a natural symptom responding to a spiritual condition. There is no kind of physical ailment in the body classified as old age. We must go back and look more closely or deeply in our family tree to discover what is hidden or kept secret. This is the determining factor of what is already manifesting or what will surface in the future. As you seek and search out the truth, find out why every child has experienced or is expected to encounter a certain kind of dark intrusion in a family.

There are things known that are not discussed in the family, things kept secret. Because they are secrets, each child grows up without a counter opportunity or power of choice to fight back. The sin in life has already been chosen for them. These are false identifiers because someone left the door open, and allowed or accepted an appetite not given them by God. Is this not the reality of Adam in the life of humanity as a whole? He opened the door to sin and the enemy seized the moment. This is how these hereditary diseases, appetites or encounters attach themselves. It is not until we move beyond this, and the curse of Adam is broken, that life has a fighting chance.

It is the principle of sowing and reaping set in motion as a consequence of our choice. We can see this play out so clearly in the life of King David when he conspired to have Uriah killed to cover up his adultery with Uriah's wife, Bathsheba. The word of the LORD came to him through Nathan the prophet that, because of this sin, the sword would never leave his house (2 Samuel 12:10-11), and indeed there was violence and tragedy within his household. You see, although God forgave him his sin, it had a direct consequence on David and his posterity.

First there was the mental anguish when he realized the gravity of his sin, which he confesses in Psalm 51:3, *"For I acknowledge my transgressions: and my sin is ever before me."* The child he had with Bathsheba died soon after birth. Then there was rape and incest when Ammon, his eldest son, forced himself on his half sister, Tamar; for this act, Absalom, his younger, took revenge and killed him (2 Samuel 15). Absalom later rebelled against his father, slept with David's concubines, and attempted to seize the throne, meeting with an untimely death. Later, a younger son, Adonijah, tried to wrest the throne from Solomon, David's appointed successor, and was executed by Solomon (1 Kings 1; 2:24).

We clearly see how the sins of the fathers become the sins of the sons. In David's case, the spirit of lust, adultery, conniving and murder was passed to the bloodline. So it is in our lives, when we open the door to sinful behavior and model it before our children. God forgives these sins when we confess them but the iniquity we have handed down to posterity must be dealt with individually. Note how God proclaimed Himself to Moses at Sinai:

> *The* LORD *God, merciful and gracious, longsuffering, and abundant in goodness and truth, Keeping mercy for thousands, forgiving iniquity and transgression and sin, and that will by no means clear the guilty;* **visiting the iniquity of the fathers upon the children, and upon the children's children, unto the third and to the fourth** (Exodus 34:10-11, emphasis added).

So often we see similar traits, patterns of behavior and conditions generation after generation, identified as poverty, depression, single-parent homes, sexual misconduct, alcoholism, drug abuse, and anger. I can recall inquiring of the Lord concerning a particular family—not in a judgmental or condemning way—but from a compassionate concern. I noticed unusual poverty in the lives of the parents and their children. He spoke to me and said, "It was because the father used financial blessings received from Him and heaped them upon the lust of his flesh." When he did this, it opened his life and the lives of his children to poverty. In the same way that DNA and physical attributes are inherited, positive or negative character traits are passed down.

However, there is hope for us as believers in Christ (Galatians 5:1). Once we can identify the flaw in character or deed in our family tree through the work and ministry of the Holy Spirit, we are empowered to be delivered and separated from the generational curse.

This is what Christ paid and secured for us. These false identifiers can be demolished because Jesus came to destroy the works of the devil through atonement on the cross. He annihilated what holds or binds us against our will by intrusion. We now have a fair chance at life, however, only a certain kind of life: one hidden in Him. This is the only hope for humankind, the only viable way to a better life. We must live, move, and have our being in Him. As believers we are to be sealed in Christ through the in-dwelling Holy Spirit until His return. On our part we must do our due diligence to search for false identifiers that restrain the physical body and human character from operating at their best according to godly biblical principles.

This leads us to the next question: how can I be right before God?

Chapter 5

RIGHTEOUSNESS

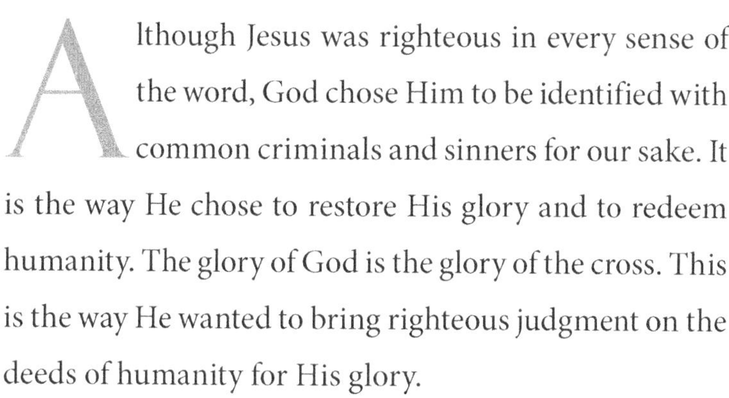

Although Jesus was righteous in every sense of the word, God chose Him to be identified with common criminals and sinners for our sake. It is the way He chose to restore His glory and to redeem humanity. The glory of God is the glory of the cross. This is the way He wanted to bring righteous judgment on the deeds of humanity for His glory.

The Self-righteous Mentality

We are of no use to God or His kingdom until we come to a proper understanding of our belief in His Son. All human efforts and merits are to no avail. The work we do for God in the hope of attaining righteousness as our way to paying such an insurmountable debt, counts for nothing. We can never repay that debt. All that is required of us is belief in Jesus—and that is sufficient to silence all the works of humanity. This is where all self-work comes to its futile end. The self-righteousness of man has no merit. This is where Jesus lost the battle and won the war. He had to die to self to complete the process of atonement, and our only response is to believe.

> *Then they said unto him, what shall we do that we might work the works of God? Jesus answered and said unto to them, this is the work of God, that ye **believe on him whom he had sent*** (John 6:28-29, emphasis added).

This is where self-righteousness comes to the end of the road in the life of every believer—the end of all human striving. We can do no righteous work to be made righteous before God. It is only through our faith in God that we are made righteous. Humanity and its longing for righteousness by doing good works in and of themselves, is nothing but vanity. They are futile and of no value because they can never settle the sin issue in themselves, only the cross can.

Of course, this makes no sense at all to our rational minds. But God uses the foolish things to confound the wise.

> *But God hath chosen the foolish things of*
> *the world to confound the wise; and God*
> *hath chosen the weak things of the world*
> *to confound the things which are mighty;*
> *And base things of the world, and things*
> *which are despised, hath God chosen, yea,*
> *and things which are not, to bring to nought*
> *things that are: That no flesh should glory*
> *in his presence* (1 Corinthians 1:27-29).

Humanity can come to salvation only through belief in Jesus. Why so? Because man can never try to take credit for his salvation; he cannot ever boast of what he did for God. No, salvation is a gift from God and all we have to do is receive it.

> *But as many received him, he gave them*
> *the power to become sons of God, even to*
> *those who believe in his name: which were*
> *born, not of the blood, nor the will of the*

flesh, nor the will of man, but of God (John 1:11-13).

But man is often driven by pride. If he could on his own merit save himself, he would try to set up his throne to be "like God." He would secure his redemption on his own based on his own achievements and "righteous acts."

The only way to enlightenment is not to strive for such righteousness but to stay in faith. That is the only righteous posture with God. Without faith, it is impossible to please God. Our merits and efforts are useless because they do not have the slightest capacity to make us right before Him. With all our human devices, all we can offer is an outward show of works masking an inward lack of obedience and faith. But does God approve of such a way? Take, for example, Saul who offered works to God by way of sacrifice, and God rejected them and him because that was the proper role of the priest (1 Samuel 13). Saul's self-serving efforts were seen as disobedience to Him. David, on the other hand, had the right understanding of sacrifice when he wrote,

The sacrifices of God are a broken spirit,
A broken and a contrite heart—These, O
God, You will not despise (Psalm 51:17).

The Weight of the Cross

Let us now try to understand the magnitude of God's redemption plan. Here was Jesus, a man who had no iota of sin in Him. Can you imagine the quality of His life—how beautiful it must have been to walk in absolute righteousness before God without a conscience stained with guilt! Yet, He suffered the ignominy of a transgressor, hanging there naked on the cross, in shame and disgrace in the sight of all.

The prophet Isaiah vividly takes us to the scene:

He is despised and rejected by men,
A Man of sorrows and acquainted with
grief.
And we hid, as it were, our faces
from Him;
He was despised, and we did not
esteem Him.

Surely He has borne our griefs

And carried our sorrows;

Yet we esteemed Him stricken,

Smitten by God, and afflicted.

But He was wounded for our transgres-

sions,

He was bruised for our iniquities;

The chastisement for our peace was

upon Him,

And by His stripes we are healed.

All we like sheep have gone astray;

We have turned, every one, to his

own way;

And the Lord *has laid on Him the iniq-*

uity of us all.

He was oppressed and He was afflicted,

Yet He opened not His mouth;

He was led as a lamb to the slaughter,

And as a sheep before its shearers is silent,

So He opened not His mouth (Isaiah

53:3-7 NKJV).

Jesus could not in any way identify with sin … that is,
until He was put on the cross and made sin for us.

Yet it pleased the Lord *to bruise Him;*
He has put Him to grief.
When You make His soul an offering
for sin,
He shall see His seed, He shall
prolong His days,
And the pleasure of the Lord *shall pros-*
per in His hand.
He shall see the labor of His soul, and be
satisfied.
By His knowledge My righteous Servant
shall justify many,
For He shall bear their iniquities ...

Because He poured out His soul unto
death,
And He was numbered with the trans-
gressors,
And He bore the sin of many,
And made intercession for the
transgressors
(Isaiah 53:10-11, 12 NKJV).

Through all that suffering even to death, Jesus had absolute confidence in His Father that He would not forsake

Him. All the false accusations, being beaten, smitten, battered, rejected, despised—all that was hurled at Him in the natural and spiritual realm—would not separate Him from the love of the Father, for this was the Plan.

His soul travailed for humanity's transgression to satisfy God's wrath. But that wrath was directed at sin with the purpose of restoring humanity to right standing with a holy God. Jesus bore the brunt of our sins when He poured out His soul unto death for us. His love was so reckless, so without restraint that He submitted Himself to the humiliation of being numbered with the transgressors. When He said, "It is finished," He was saying to Father God, "I have finished the work You gave Me to do concerning humanity. I followed the path. They are made righteous with You through faith in Me. Just as Abraham believed Your promise to Him and was made righteous, if they will but believe in Me, they will be made righteous as well."

Although Jesus was innocent of any wrongdoing to the civil state or religious system and had all the power to free Himself, yet He surrendered Himself meekly like a lamb going to the slaughter. He did not open His mouth to defend Himself in the eyes of man because He knew it was more important to stand righteous before God. This was infinitely more valuable to Him than His ego or public reputation.

So all that pressing was for us. The Bible says "it pleased the Father" to bruise Jesus because many would be made righteous because of Him. Many would receive redemption for their sins because of what He endured. And so, the will of the Lord reached total fulfillment in His hand. What is the will of God for your life? Know what your Savior endured, and it will explain the suffering you go through.

These are His silent words to you explaining the reason for His sacrifice. "Everything that has happened is being used to further My plan for your life. It may appear like it is the enemy's hour of triumph but this is only allowed because of what I know concerning your future and what I have called you to. For I know My thoughts toward you," says the Lord, "thoughts of peace to give you a glorious end. You can go through life secure in Me if you understand this principle, and embrace it. The end I expect for you is not the one you planned for yourself but what I intend to be at work concerning your life. This is how I permit what happens in your life. You see, the plans

I have for you are good plans to prosper you, to keep you, and to heal you." (Jeremiah 29:11)

The Lord continues, "All the while, My beloved Son was being crushed, mutilated, beaten, marred, disfigured, bruised, and crucified, He was in the palm of My hand. It pleased Me because I knew and understood the ultimate predetermined purpose behind it. I permitted it only because it advanced My plan. In no way should you be led to believe that the enemy had dominion over Him, or over any situation when I am in control. This is Truth speaking to you, reasoning with you, and teaching you. Satan is no more than a pawn in My hand; he is acting out the unfolding of My plan. I am the one that tries the hearts of men to purify their hearts to righteousness and weed out all wickedness from them."

Sin and its Derivatives

Before we move on, it would be a good time to pause and review a few key terms related to sin.

Sin: it comes from the Greek word *hamartia*, described in Strong's 266: as missing the mark; hence guilty of sin, or a moral failure; an offense against the moral law based on divine law.

While sin is generally seen in our acts, any thought or word considered immoral, selfish, shameful, harmful, or alienating might be termed sinful. Our sin nature causes us to naturally gravitate towards selfishness, envy, and pride, even when we are trying to do good.

Transgression: refers to presumptuous or intentional sin, when we choose to disobey God's laws just as David willfully committed adultery with Bathsheba and murder when He ordered her husband to go to the battle front.

Iniquity: is willful sin or wickedness. It describes the corrupt and immoral nature inherent in human character. Unlike "sin," which denotes the actions themselves, "iniquity" describes a distinctive character trait of the individual.

Justified: in Strong's 1342, *dikaiosis* is the act of God declaring men free from guilt and acceptable to Him. This means righteous or just; made righteous in the sight of God; the act by which God moves a person from a state of sin (unjust) to a state of grace (just).

Righteous: is acting according to divine law, free from guilt or sin, morally right, justifiable. Righteousness is the change in a willing person's condition from a state of sin to a state of right standing with God; the act of acquittal whereby God gives sinners the status of righteous.

So How Do We Attain Righteousness?

It is God who calls the sinners righteous according to His terms, not ours. He can set out the path and the conditions of this binding agreement because it is His gift. Our part is to remain in faith in believing in God to bestow righteousness upon us and to continue to abide in faith. See how Abraham believed in God, and it was credited to him as righteous.

In the book of Romans, the apostle Paul expounds on how one becomes righteous and just before God. His insights are astounding. He explains that righteousness is the fusion of the Old Testament covenant with Abraham with the New Covenant in Christ. Both are not attained by works or by adherence to the law but are entirely reliant on His grace. The unjust are called righteous before God through Christ's death for our trespasses and His resurrection for our justification. Those acts acquitted us from the law, sin, and death.

Now made righteous before God, we are reconciled with Him, and have peace and life in Christ through the Holy Spirit. Having been saved, we must continue in complete trust in Jesus by exercising our faith in Him and remaining dependent on grace. In no way is humanity qualified to contribute to justification on its own merits. It comes by grace alone appropriated by faith. This is an active faith working through love (Galatians 5:6) and we cannot allow it to become stagnant or dormant.

A Subtle Difference

Let me now share how that radical truth reached home for me—the daughter of a mighty man of God whose father was also a preacher. As a little girl, I would get up at night and hear my father weeping as he played his guitar before the Lord in worship. He fasted more than he ate; his waist was a size 27 or 28. At every service I would see miracles, signs, and great wonders: demons were cast out, and people were delivered; alcoholics would stumble under the tent and leave sober. Each night, the altar was filled with drug addicts, prostitutes, and gang members giving their hearts to Jesus.

That was my background. I grew up knowing full well the power of a consecrated life. You might say consecration was embedded in my genes. It was simply an ingrained lifestyle of trust with minimal effort. But the Lord slowly began to shift me from my good works to a life of faith, and that was the most difficult turn for me to make. You see, I knew I was consecrated before the Lord because of the lifestyle I chose to live for Him and my confidence in God came from this consecration. However, God was coming for something much more fundamental, not because it was wrong to consecrate oneself but because of how I defined my righteousness. It was works based. It was the confidence of my right standing before Him that felt threatened as He began to shift me to faith. Now, with no foundation for my confidence to rest on, I felt most inadequate because I was no longer busy earning my righteousness before Him.

To be honest, that, more properly, is self-righteousness. When my eyes were opened, I saw the filthiness of my own righteousness before Him. Now, in desperation to purge my conscience of dead works, I had to fall forward into the grace of God through faith in what Jesus did for me. I had to do away with works completely, and hold on to only the relationship. I realized that God was not focusing on the consecration because, although I was ignorant of its reality in my conscience, heart, and mind, He was not.

For a time, He honored it. He understood it was the way I knew to get to Him. However, once the relationship solidified, I was strong and mature enough to place my trust in all that His grace provided me. It is the same for all of us. Ultimately, He wants to take down the self-righteousness that blocks us from coming to Him in total brokenness, and becoming utterly dependent upon His grace so that He is truly glorified in our lives.

> *Now to him who works, the wages are not counted as grace but as debt. But to him who does not work but believes on Him who justifies the ungodly, his faith is accounted for righteousness just as David also describes the blessedness of the man to whom God imputes righteousness apart from works:*

"Blessed are those whose lawless deeds are forgiven,

And whose sins are covered;

Blessed is the man to whom the Lord

shall not impute sin" (Romans 4:4-8 NKJV).

It is faith that causes a man to believe, while it is doubt that causes him to try to reason things out. We must first believe He rewards those who diligently seek Him in faith (Hebrews 11:6). Abraham believed God, and it was this trust in Him that made him righteous in God's sight. When we approach God with the same kind of unquestioning faith, we are indeed the children of Abraham. For God who knew He would justify the Gentiles through faith, preached a message of faith to Abraham as a precursor to the gospel message, saying, "In you shall all nations be blessed."

So we who are people of faith are blessed the same way faithful Abraham was blessed. God counts the faith of a man as sufficient to declare him righteous in His eyes, for faith is the hallmark of righteousness. *"For it is with your heart that you believe and are justified, and it is with your mouth that you profess your faith and are saved*" (Romans 10:10 NIV).

You give Him faith, and He gives you back righteousness.

Abraham was made righteous because he believed in God and did not disbelieve at any moment of time. No doubt he was persuaded by his wife to father a child with her servant, but at no time did he "unconvince" himself of the promise. Nor did he exercise the right of refusal to the promises of God, unlike the children of Israel when they were in the wilderness. They exercised their right of refusal when they murmured against God when most of the spies returned from Canaan with a bad report (Numbers 13). But Abraham was steadfast in his faith. He stayed convinced concerning God, against time, against the deadness of his body and the deadness of Sarah's womb. It was as simple as this: *"And He believed the LORD, and he counted it to him for righteousness"* (Genesis 15:6).

What things are you facing that have the potential to cause you to doubt Him? This is where your frank assessment must begin. Identify the situations and the cost of ceasing to have faith. Is there anything worth giving up for not believing God? *"I said therefore unto you that ye shall die in your sins: for if ye believe not that I am he, ye shall die in your sins"* (John 8:24).

When we answer questions like these, our response is always "No, never!" However, could our deeds and plans be the exact opposite of what we confess?

So let us take stock of all the things that threaten our faith. What things or areas do you consider to be game changers for the ultimate good? Please note this is exactly where the test or trial will arise. It is the ultimate purpose that will be tried and tested. It's the one thing that could cause you to give up on Him. This is where He must be LORD. It must be an unshakeable stance. You must come to the point that you say, "I will trust and believe in Him even when circumstances turn against me and doubts assail my mind."

Some people complain they lack faith but the truth is God has given each of us a measure of faith to know and to believe in Him (Romans 12:3). His issue with His body is that He cannot get a one hundred percent guarantee on His investment. He gave us the power to become sons of God when we rise up in faith but we frustrate His grace and take advantage of the death of His Son if we fail to fully reciprocate in trust.

When you look at His mercy, grace, and goodness, it is the goodness of the Lord that leads us to repentance and not to despair. His sovereignty, His immutability, His omniscience, His omnipresence, His self-existence, His faithfulness, His love, His kindness, they all combine to build a picture of Him as faithful, steadfast and consistent. Surely that increases our security and confidence in Him!

So what have we learned about righteousness? It is right standing with God because of faith. It is here we are to position ourselves and stand to take on an offensive position as opposed to a defensive one. All of our human attempts to be self-righteous or righteousness in self are annihilated by this stance. No more fighting in my strength but learning to be strong in the Lord and the power of His might, for it is the righteousness of God. This is the covering of the flesh because, when we operate in the old nature, there is no covering. We can only access the righteousness of God through faith in Christ Jesus. This is where the benefits of atonement are accessible and available to us. We can only operate in faith to attain it. Each day, we must wake up in His righteousness and renew our trust in Him.

None of these positions is ever attainable in our own strength. Then who can we rely on?

LED BY THE SPIRIT

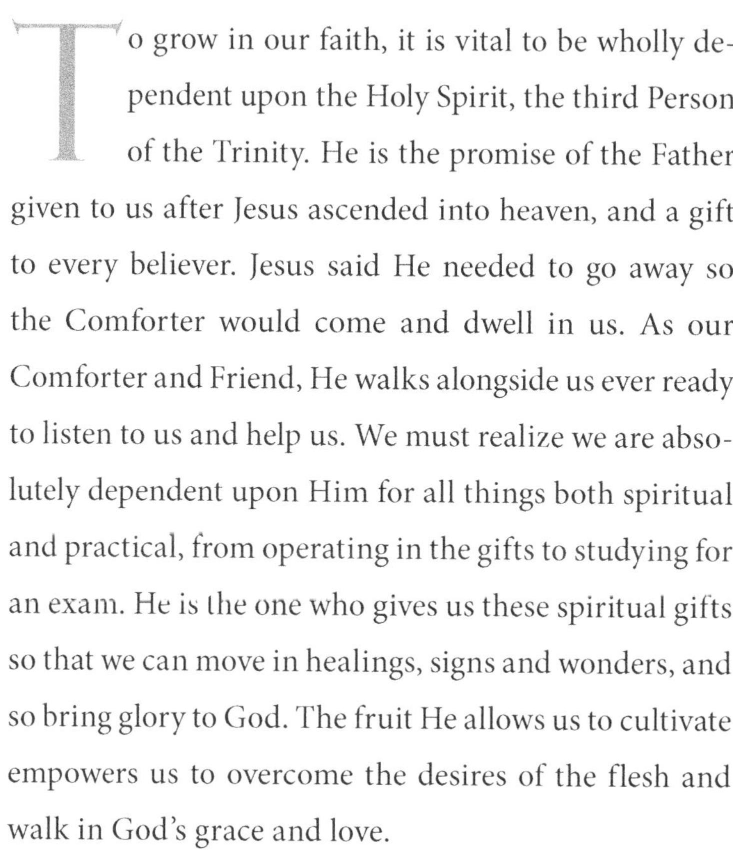

To grow in our faith, it is vital to be wholly dependent upon the Holy Spirit, the third Person of the Trinity. He is the promise of the Father given to us after Jesus ascended into heaven, and a gift to every believer. Jesus said He needed to go away so the Comforter would come and dwell in us. As our Comforter and Friend, He walks alongside us ever ready to listen to us and help us. We must realize we are absolutely dependent upon Him for all things both spiritual and practical, from operating in the gifts to studying for an exam. He is the one who gives us these spiritual gifts so that we can move in healings, signs and wonders, and so bring glory to God. The fruit He allows us to cultivate empowers us to overcome the desires of the flesh and walk in God's grace and love.

The Holy Spirit indwells every believer and equips us with wisdom, knowledge, and understanding to succeed in all God has for us to accomplish. While natural things according to the wisdom of this age appeal to the carnal or fleshly, He gives us fresh desires to live at a higher level by being led by His promptings and obeying His word. We abide in the Word through the power and presence of the Holy Spirit, just as Jesus abided in the Father when He was here on earth. As our Teacher and the Spirit of Truth, He enlightens our minds with revelations of the Word and brings to remembrance the things we learned. He leads and guides us into all truth and will never say anything contrary to the word of God.

From Children to Sons

As born-again believers, we are children of God and our close walk with the Holy Spirit will bring about the transformation towards sonship. This enables us to mature in spiritual things and develop the character to carry the anointing upon us. For this to take place, we have to continually renew our minds with the Word. This will bring greater understanding of the ways of God and our new identity with its characteristics. As soon as we are born again our spirit becomes the perfected part of us, while the soul and body are being renewed. It is a day by day, moment by moment process. At first, the old unrenewed nature will try to dominate our thoughts and actions but we must let our spirit take the lead.

Be assured the Holy Spirit is committed to doing this work in us. The more we yield to His promptings, the more in-tune we will be with the ways of God. The more we know Him, the more we give Him space to work in us to will to do all of His good pleasure.

Our spiritual journey did not begin with works and neither will it end with works lest any man should boast of his achievements. No, it is only by the Spirit of God that we will see a changed life that displays all the fruit of His Spirit. The old nature is now dead and we are alive to Christ, no longer living a life that is pleasing to the flesh but one that is pleasing to the Lord. At salvation, every believer is endowed with the fruit of the Spirit but it is our responsibility to nurture them through practice and the Word. It's an ongoing process that has to be cultivated before the life of Christ is truly seen in our character.

The dynamics at work here is the exchange of our carnal will with the desires of our spirit which seeks the things of God. This is why we need to offer up our will to God each day. If we genuinely want to put to death the flesh, the process of developing maturity will be sweet. If not, it will be a very bitter experience. The biggest war will be the pull of the flesh against the Spirit. We win when we yield to the Holy Spirit and not to our flesh. Nevertheless, He understands our weaknesses, and has committed to showing us a way of escape for every temptation that overwhelms us. But we must do our part to resist the temptation and draw from Him strength to endure and overcome.

We often assume that our character is typically tested where we lose the battle. But it is also when we win the war against our carnality that we are in danger of giving in to pride. We must therefore put on the shield of faith to resist the fiery darts of the enemy (Ephesians 6:16). To be an overcomer, we must literally eat the word of God, that is, search out, meditate on, and apply His word and will for our life. Be aware that the adversary knows the Word even better than you—even though he does not submit to it—and he will appear as an angel of light to twist the Word at every chance he gets just as he deceived Eve.

But we exercise wisdom when we know our righteous standing is only in Christ and are not ignorant of the character flaws that hinder our continuous growth. The areas we should focus on to solidify God's presence in our life are: assurance of His unconditional love for us and His commitment to help us grow in all things that pertain to life and godliness. The Holy Spirit teaches us how to safeguard our heart by seeing reality from God's perspective and not according to how we are often taught or judge things. The danger is in making our heart the final arbiter because it is often our greatest deceiver, and completely untrustworthy.

> *The heart is deceitful above all things, And desperately wicked; Who can know it? I, the LORD, search the heart, I test the mind, Even to give every man according to his ways, According to the fruit of his doings* (Jeremiah 17:9-10 NKJV).

The Holy Spirit is every ready to speak into our spirits if we cooperate with Him in the renewal process, and bring every stray thought and imagination into subjection to Him. We must resolve to take on the mind of Christ daily by reading, studying and continuously meditating on His Word.

Discerning of Spirits

Do you know that two people may declare the same thing but it is the Holy Spirit that causes us to discern whose statement to receive? One of the nine gifts of the Holy Spirit is the ability to discern the spirit behind a character or act, whether good or evil.

Let me illustrate this from the book of Acts where Paul and his team were ministering in Philippi. Every day they were followed by a slave girl loudly touting them as servants of the Most High God:

> *As we were going to the place of prayer, we were met by a slave girl who had a spirit of divination and brought her owners much gain by fortune-telling. She followed Paul and us, crying out, "These men are servants of the Most High God, who proclaim to you the way of salvation." And this she kept doing for many days. Paul, having become greatly annoyed, turned and said to the spirit, "I command you in the name of Jesus Christ to come out of her." And it came out that very hour (Acts 16:16-18 ESV).*

One could ask why Paul was so offended. After all, the girl, even though she operated in fortune-telling, was speaking the truth and in a sense acknowledging their high calling. It could even be considered as some kind of promotion for these evangelists who were new to the region. Again, why did Paul only react after a few days, and not immediately?

The answer is in the proper exercising of the gift of the discerning of spirits. At first, Paul may have been annoyed because her loud cries were disruptively calling attention to herself. Moreover, he did not want to be associated with her kind of trade. But that was at the human level. He did not react at once because he was likely seeking the Holy Spirit for the right response. That response finally came when his own spirit became "greatly annoyed" (Greek *diaponetheis*)—some translations say "distressed" or "greatly offended"—and he could confidently identify the evil spirit in her and command it to leave.

This passage highlights two important principles. The first is that the word of God needs no promotion or endorsement from the kingdom of darkness. It bears witness to itself with its own signs and wonders. The second is not to receive its message even though it appears to be speaking the truth.

Jesus showed us what to do in the first chapter of Mark. When He was in the synagogue, He was confronted by a man possessed by an unclean spirit. The spirit in the man recognized Him:

> *"Why are you interfering with us, Jesus of Nazareth? Have you come to destroy us? I know who you are—the Holy One of God!"*
>
> *But Jesus reprimanded him. "Be quiet! Come out of the man," he ordered. At that, the evil spirit screamed, threw the man into a convulsion, and then came out of him* (Mark 1:23-25 NLT).

The lesson is never to engage in conversation with an evil spirit; just rebuke it and cast it out.

The Apostle Paul summarizes our stance when we can discern the spirit behind the scene whether it be the smooth-talk of politicians, the claims of advertisers or the revelations of new agers. Reject the message outright and rebuke the spirit (under your breath, if in public). Do not receive it, no matter how good it sounds—unless you want the extra baggage that comes with it.

> *Don't team up with those who are unbe-lievers. How can righteousness be a partner with wickedness? How can light live with darkness?* (2 Corinthians 6:14 NLT)

It's Your Choice

At the end of the day, there are only two choices here on earth: to walk in the Spirit or after the flesh. No man can serve two masters, for he will hate the one and love the other. The fruit of our lives will display the choice we made, and show to whom we have yielded our members. Remember, we are in this world but not of this world. Once we have the proper perspective, we can fully grasp the spirit behind everything in the world. What the world serves caters to a lifestyle led by the carnal mind with its passions and lusts. All that it feeds is the desire of the flesh, the lust of the eyes, and the pride of life in its cravings. It moves towards sensual gratification, the insatiable longings of the mind, and the pride in one's human resources or earthly things.

But the Holy Spirit will show us how our lust for the things of this world is stirred up and driven by the enemy. It is Satan who draws us out of the realm of the Spirit back to the carnal mindset. Why? So he can manipulate, seduce, and control us. How? By infiltrating our thought life with his doubts and imaginations in order to separate us from God. The battle is in and for the mind. But God wants us to be led by the Spirit, to possess the mind of Christ, and walk in the fruit of the Spirit. These are the keys to overcoming the love of the world and all its offerings. Satan wants our minds "dumbed-down" to operating in the sensual, and to consider this normal. He feeds the senses and their cravings to keep us hankering after the enticements of the flesh that the world so readily supplies.

In conclusion, know that every choice we make will reproduce after its kind. So which god will we serve? Do we decide to live after the self, the flesh, and the love of the world? As Solomon, so eloquently stated in Ecclesiastes, everything in life is temporal and filled with vanity. It will all fade away like a breath. Wasn't this the same gift that Satan offered Eve—to eat and become wise? But what was locked within this gift was a curse that enslaved people—to sin, fear, sickness, death, doubt, and the burden of the law. Sorrow comes to us because it is a part of the curse upon humanity.

Rest in Him

The good news is that we have Jesus to come to and obtain rest. What He did on the cross paid for the brunt of the law, and the curse of sin and death. He is again inviting all who struggle:

> *"Come to me all who labor and are heavy laden, and I will give you rest. Take my yoke upon you, and learn from me, for I am gentle and lowly in heart, and you will find rest for your souls. For my yoke is easy, and my burden is light"* (Matthew 11:28-30 ESV).

The yoke of sin—the sorrow and weariness and of the soul—is abolished in Jesus. Find rest and peace for the soul in Jesus. The revelation of who He is comes through our own suffering. Paul willingly endured his trials for the privilege of knowing Christ and thereby sharing in His glory:

> *I have suffered the loss of all things and count them as rubbish, in order that I may gain Christ and be found in him, not having a righteousness of my own that comes from the law, but that which comes through faith in Christ, the righteousness from God that depends on faith—that I may know him and the power of his resurrection, and may share his sufferings, becoming like him in his death, that by any means possible I may attain the resurrection from the dead* (Philippians 3:8-11 ESV).

And, like Paul, I too gladly accept my suffering for the excellence and beauty of knowing Him. What a minimal cost to know Jesus!

As we bring this narrative to a close, I want to again lay emphasis on Satan's utter hatred for humanity because he knows we are the object of God's affection. He did not set out to be like God because some trace of good remained in him. No, he was completely depraved and his goal was to supplant his Creator. We must come to recognize this enemy of both God and man. He has no good intentions towards any of us, so do not be fooled by his sugar-coated words. All that he guarantees is to aid in your destruction and that of humanity at large. As an angel of light, his power comes from us believing the lie.

But there is no reason to fear, when we come to know, trust, and believe we are the object of God's affection. God's perfect love is ours to receive and enjoy freely. And—I'll say it again—redemption is necessary because we are rebels bound by sin and unable to save ourselves. But because of His love, He reconciled us to Himself while we were yet sinners without virtue or merit.

> *But as many as received him, to them gave he power to become the sons of God, even to them that believe on his name: Which were born, not of blood, nor of the will of the flesh, nor of the will of man, but of God. And the Word was made flesh, and dwelt among us, (and we beheld his glory, the glory as of the only begotten of the Father,) full of grace and truth* (John 1:12-14).

He is the Redeemer of humankind, our answer to every situation we face. What a beautiful love story when we simply take Him at His Word!

Notes

Merriam-Webster online dictionary & onlineThesaurus.com

Matthew Henry Commentary on The Whole Bible – New Modern Edition Complete and Unabridged in six volumes Copyright @1991 by Hendrickson Publishers, Inc. Seventh Printing – January 2003

Dakes Annotated Reference Bible The Old and New Testament, with notes, Concordance and Index @ Copyright holders Melanie Dake, Edward Finnis Dake, Monique Germaine, Kimberly Dake Kennedy, Kathryn Dake Iglinksi and Dake Ministries Lawrenceville, Georgia KJV Edition @ Copyright 2014 Fifth Printing – December 2019

Wikipedia The Free Encyclopedia www..wikipedia.com

Oxford Languages | The Home of Language Data (oup.com)

http://www.earnestangley.org/read/article/seducing_spirits

Author Contact Information

You may contact the author at:
2008 Airline Drive, Ste. 300 #202
Bossier City, LA 71111

Email: admin@thlministries.org
www.thlministries.org
phone: 318-918-9248

Made in the USA
Monee, IL
07 July 2026